Table of Contents

	Preface	5
I	Introduction: Some Reasons for the Mitzvah of Shemittah	7
II	History: How Shemittah Was Kept Over the Years	12
III	Shemittah Laws	21
IV	Shemittah: In Eretz Yisrael	31
V	Shemittah: Outside Eretz Yisrael	47
VI	Shemittas Kesafim: Financial Shemittah	49
VII	Conclusion	51
VIII	Questions About Shemittah	54

SHEMITTAH:
What It's All About

SHEMITTAH:
What It's All About

Compiled by
Rabbi Eliezer Gevirtz
Prepared for publication by
Rabbi Yaakov Fruchter

In Dedication

This publication is sponsored by
Mr. John Saunders
of Sydney, Australia, in honor of
Rabbi Menachem Gottesman,
on the occasion of his receiving
The Maurice and Golde Rothman
Memorial Torah Leadership Award
at the 49th Annual Dinner of Torah Umesorah –
The National Society for Hebrew Day Schools –
January 24, 1993 – 2 Shvat 5753.

"For the Jewish community to have such excellent, devoted and selfless ambassadors as Rabbi and Mrs. Menachem Gottesman, is a great honor to us all. They give their love and care to so many people without reservation. To have our children in the hands of such a wonderful couple is a blessing indeed, because our children are our most precious commodity."

John Saunders
Sydney, Australia

Torah Umesorah Publications

ISBN: 0-914131-78-8
Copyright © 1993
Torah Umesorah Publications
5723 Eighteenth Avenue
Brooklyn, N.Y. 11204
718-259-1223 • Fax 718-259-1795

בס"ד

Preface

We are pleased to present this publication, "Shemittah: What It's All About"—for students and teachers. Its purpose is to make the subject of *Shemittah* more meaningful for its readers by offering them a brief overview and simple explanation of the background of the *mitzvah*, some "do's and dont's," and a look at how this *mitzvah* is observed today in *Eretz Yisrael*. *It is not meant to be a guide to the laws of Shemittah.* These laws are much too complex to be treated comprehensively between the covers of such a booklet.

The *Shemittah* year provides an excellent opportunity to teach our students about the *mitzvos* of *Eretz Yisrael* and to imbue them with true *ahavas Eretz Yisrael*. It creates a greater appreciation for *kedushas ha'aretz*, which in turn fosters the realization that every spadeful of earth in *Eretz Yisrael* is holy.

Because of their unequivocal faith and trust in Hashem, the *Shemittah*-keepers are referred to as גִּבֹּרֵי כֹחַ עֹשֵׂי דְבָרוֹ. "Mighty men of power, doers of His word." And because of their unyielding devotion to this *mitzvah*, Hashem's promise to them is unequivocal as well: וְצִוִּיתִי אֶת בִּרְכָתִי לָכֶם בַּשָּׁנָה הַשִּׁשִּׁית וְעָשָׂת אֶת הַתְּבוּאָה לִשְׁלֹשׁ הַשָּׁנִים. "I will command my blessing upon you in the sixth year, and it shall bring forth fruit for three years."

The lessons learnt from the *Shemittah*-keepers in particular, and the *Shemittah* year in general can be used effectively to instill and strengthen *bitachon* and *emunah* among us all. Let us make the most of this special year.

We want to thank all those who lent a helping hand in the preparation of this booklet. The time and effort they gave for the project is truly appreciated.

May the merit of keeping and learning about the *mitzvah* of *Shemittah* bring us a step closer to the coming of *Mashiach*, as our *Chazal* state: בְּמוֹצָאֵי שְׁבִיעִית בֶּן דָּוִד בָּא.

Rabbi Yaakov Fruchter
Director,
Torah Umesorah Publications

Farmers in Eretz Yisrael work hard in their fields for six years.

I. Introduction: Some Reasons for the Mitzvah of Shemittah

If you think about it, you'll realize that we are blessed with many gifts during our lives. This means more than the presents we get on happy occasions and the rewards we get for good work. Everything we own—as well as the air we breathe and the food we eat—is also a gift. All of these things come our way due to Hashem's kindness.

People use their ownership in different ways. Some people are very generous. They share their possessions with their family, their friends and the needy. Other people, however, grow greedy. They feel that they created their good fortune, and so they think that they—and only they—should benefit from it. Sometimes, they buy only the best for themselves and pay no attention to the needs of others. And sometimes they hoard their wealth, thinking they will keep it forever. They forget that Hashem granted them this wealth, and that He has many ways to take it away.

The word *Shemittah* means to withdraw ownership. The *Shemittah* year reminds us that Hashem owns the world and everything in it, and that whatever we own is given to us by Him. The *mitzvah* of *Shemittah* refers to not working the land in *Eretz Yisrael* every seventh year. In the seventh year, farmers in *Eretz Yisrael* withdraw from their control over the crops of the land and leave them free for anyone who wants, to take. The *mitzvah* is first mentioned in the Torah in *Parshas Mishpatim* (*Shemos* 23:10–11):

וְשֵׁשׁ שָׁנִים תִּזְרַע אֶת אַרְצֶךָ, וְאָסַפְתָּ אֶת תְּבוּאָתָהּ. וְהַשְּׁבִיעִת תִּשְׁמְטֶנָּה וּנְטַשְׁתָּהּ וְאָכְלוּ אֶבְיֹנֵי עַמֶּךָ וְיִתְרָם תֹּאכַל חַיַּת הַשָּׂדֶה, כֵּן תַּעֲשֶׂה לְכַרְמְךָ לְזֵיתֶךָ.

"Six years you shall plant your land and harvest its produce. But in the seventh you shall let it rest and lie fallow (uncultivated); the poor among your people may eat it, and what they leave, the beasts of the field shall eat. You shall do the same with your vineyard and your olive tree."

The Torah provides more details of this *mitzvah* in *Parshas Behar*, (*Vayikra* 25: 2–5):

...דַּבֵּר אֶל בְּנֵי יִשְׂרָאֵל וְאָמַרְתָּ אֲלֵהֶם כִּי תָבֹאוּ אֶל הָאָרֶץ אֲשֶׁר אֲנִי נֹתֵן לָכֶם, וְשָׁבְתָה הָאָרֶץ שַׁבָּת לַה'. שֵׁשׁ שָׁנִים תִּזְרַע שָׂדֶךָ וְשֵׁשׁ שָׁנִים תִּזְמֹר כַּרְמֶךָ, וְאָסַפְתָּ אֶת תְּבוּאָתָהּ. וּבַשָּׁנָה הַשְּׁבִיעִת שַׁבַּת שַׁבָּתוֹן יִהְיֶה לָאָרֶץ שַׁבָּת לַה', שָׂדְךָ לֹא תִזְרָע וְכַרְמְךָ לֹא תִזְמֹר. אֵת סְפִיחַ קְצִירְךָ לֹא תִקְצוֹר וְאֶת עִנְּבֵי נְזִירֶךָ לֹא תִבְצֹר, שְׁנַת שַׁבָּתוֹן יִהְיֶה לָאָרֶץ.

7

"Speak to the Children of Israel and say to them, 'When you come to the land that I am giving you, the land will keep a Sabbath for Hashem. Six years you shall plant your field and six years you shall prune your vineyard and harvest its produce. But in the seventh year, there will be a Sabbath of solemn rest for the land, a Sabbath for Hashem. Your field you shall not plant and your vineyard you shall not prune. Whatever grows of itself from your harvest you shall not reap, and the grapes of your vine you shall not gather. It is to be a year of solemn rest for the land.' "

We observe *mitzvos* whether or not we understand the reasons for them. The fact that Hashem commanded us to keep them, is enough reason for us to do so. Some Sages attempted to explain certain *mitzvos* to us, so that they can be more understandable. However, each *mitzvah* has many more reasons that were never revealed to us. In this context let us discuss the *mitzvah* of *Shemittah*.

The *pesukim* (sentences) just mentioned speak of the land keeping a Sabbath for Hashem. Some commentators (such as *Rambam*) explain that letting the fields lie fallow (uncultivated) is very beneficial for them. They then produce better crops during the coming years. In fact, bitter experiences like the problem of the area in the United States that became known as the Dust Bowl during the 1930's, is one example which shows this to be a reality. One of the reasons that the land stopped being fertile was that most farmers used to plant their fields year after year without a rest, trying to get them to yield as many crops as possible. But this removed many of the minerals from the ground, and caused valuable topsoil to turn into dust in which nothing grew. The farmers learned to let their fields lie fallow for awhile, so that the all-important soil nutrients could be restored. Then, the crops were more fruitful in future years. The land needs a rest just as living things do.

Other Sages teach that the *mitzvah* of *Shemittah* was given for reasons other than agricultural considerations. Like all *mitzvos* of the Torah, it provides us with lessons that help make us a holier people. *Shemittah* calls attention to the allegience Jews must pay to Hashem as Master of the world, and to the assistance we must give our fellow man.

Rabbi Avraham Ibn Ezra and Rabbi Moshe ben Nachman (*Ramban*), each in his own way, note the similarities between the *Shemittah* cycle and the holy Shabbos, and allude to their deeper meanings. However, let us try to understand the similarities on a more basic level.

Think of Shabbos for a moment. If you've experienced a true Shabbos, you'll know that it's a special day—a holy time devoted to spirituality. We do not work or carry on our usual everyday activities. Instead, we dedicate extra time to our prayers, to our learning, and to our families. Why? First of all, Shabbos reminds us of Hashem's control over the world. When we rest, we remember that Hashem also "rested" after creating the world in six days. We Jews must follow His ways and copy His example. By doing this, we acknowledge that Hashem is our Master and Guide, and that we are His subjects. For six days each week we show our control, our mastery of the world. And on the seventh day we hand that control back to Hashem.

Secondly, Shabbos also reminds us that life is not meant just for rushing off to work to earn more and more money. There is a higher purpose for our existence. We are here to gain spiritual greatness, to become as close to Hashem as possible. By studying and following the Torah, we become loving, caring individuals who devote our lives to doing good deeds. When we keep the Shabbos faithfully, we remember to dedicate ourselves to Hashem.

The laws of *Shemittah* serve a similar purpose. Farmers in *Eretz Yisrael* work hard for six years. They plant their fields, harvest their crops, and earn what they need. Sometimes they—like others—may think that whatever grows is the result of their own skill, that they are fully entitled to everything they produce. They may even take their success for granted, and forget the One Who really caused it all to grow. (See *Kli Yakar—Parshas Behar*.)

Then comes the seventh year— the *Shemittah* year. The farmers are forbidden to do their usual work. Their skills are of no use, and they have to survive on what Hashem gives them. They are reminded of the truth: it is Hashem Who really created and owns the land, Who controls its produce and the farmers' destiny. They are only the temporary tenants of the land, and the crops they raise are only gifts from the Alm-ghty.

The *Shemittah* year not only gives the land a rest, it also gives the farmers free time. As on Shabbos, they have more time to spend on Torah learning and family affairs— more time to consider the purposes of life. When they resume work the next year, they are more thankful to Hashem for what they produce, and they use the fruits of their labors for the right purposes.

In days of old, when a large percentage of the population worked as farmers, the sight of so many Jews stopping their work to sanctify Hashem's Name was truly inspiring. Rabbi Samson Raphael Hirsch, in his commentary to *Parshas Behar* (*Vayikra* 25:5), makes the following observation:

> If we picture to ourselves the carrying out of the *Sheviis* (*Shemittah*) laws, they present to our minds a most wonderful yearlong act of homage performed by a whole nation, where every field and orchard, every garden and meadow, every fruit, every blade of grass is made to proclaim that G-d and G-d alone, is the L-rd and owner of the Land. Dutifully laying the whole territory at His feet, the inhabitants have to consider themselves as mere *geirim* (strangers) and *toshavim* (dwellers), as tolerated tenants of the land. Stripped of all haughtiness and pride of possession, (they) retire before G-d in complete equality with the same rights as the poorest inhabitants and the animals of the wild.

The fields getting their rest on the seventh year—the Shemittah year.

Naturally, the thought of leaving a field untended for an entire year can be frightening. The Torah anticipates the people's fears: "And if you will say, 'What will we eat in the seventh year? Behold, we cannot plant and we cannot gather in our produce.'" (*Vayikra* 25:20). The answer of Hashem comes in the very next *pesukim* (sentences): "Then I will command My blessing upon you in the sixth year, and (the land) will yield produce for the three years. And you will plant in the eighth year, and eat of the old produce until the ninth year." (*Vayikra* 25:21-2). If the Jews show their faith in Hashem by keeping the *Shemittah*, He will show His love for them by providing enough crops in the sixth year to last for the sixth, seventh, and eighth years. Then the crops of the eighth year will be available for eating during the ninth year.

Those who observe *Shemittah* according to the Torah are true heroes of faith. Rabbi Yitzchak said that the *pasuk*, "*Gibborey ko'ach osey devoro*"—"mighty men of power, doers of His word"—refers to those who keep the *Shemittah* laws. "It is customary for a man to do a *mitzvah* for an entire day, for a whole week, or even for a month," Rabbi Yitzchak explained, "but who can do so for an entire year? It is only the *Shemittah* observer who can do this, for he sees his field lie fallow, his vineyard untended, and pays his tax [to the government] in silence for the entire *Shemittah* year. Is there a mightier man than he?"

On the other hand, there is a stiff punishment if the Jewish nation does not keep *Shemittah*. The *Mishnah* in *Avos* (5:9) states that "exile comes upon the world for idoaltry, immorality, bloodshed and *for not allowing the soil to rest in the* Shemittah *year*." The source of this statement is the Torah: "Then the land will enjoy her Sabbaths as long as she lies desolate, and you will be in your enemies' land" (*Vayikra* 26:34). The punishment is harsh, but it makes sense. If the Jews do not have enough trust in Hashem to stop working during the seventh year, then they do not deserve His protection. And if they do not give *Eretz Yisrael* its due rest, then they are not worthy of living in that land, and so Hashem sends them into exile.

Today, the majority of Jews do not own farms. Nevertheless, with millions of Jews living in *Eretz Yisrael*, the laws and lessons of *Shemittah* are still very applicable. The year 5754 (1993-94) is a *Shemittah* year, and the laws of *Shemittah* have a great effect on how Jewish farmers and consumers both in and outside of Israel conduct their lives during this time. This booklet will help you become familiar with the observances and the importance of the *Shemittah* year. If we comply fully with the laws and the messages they convey, we can expect Hashem to reward our trust in Him and allow us to live in peace and purity in *Eretz Yisrael*.

II. History: How Shemittah Was Kept Over the Years

The 40-year journey in the desert was finally over. The people's beloved leader, Moshe Rabbeinu, was no longer there to guide them. Almost all the people who had been taken out of Egypt in a blaze of miracles were no longer alive. But there was a new, courageous leader named Yehoshua, and Hashem had ordered him to lead the people into the Promised Land.

The settlement of *Eretz Yisrael* was far from easy. Yehoshua and the Jews had to conquer most of the cities one by one. It took seven long years, but with the aid of Hashem's miracles, even such well-fortified cities as Yericho and Chatzor were captured. Then came the task of dividing up the land among the members of the twelve tribes. This, too, took seven years. At last, the holy people were at home in the Holy Land and the Torah commanded that this was when the complete fulfillment of all the land-related *mitzvos* in the Torah should take place. So it was time to begin the *Shemittah* cycle. After six years, on *Rosh Hashanah* of the Hebrew New Year 2509 (almost 3,247 years ago), the first *Shemittah* year was proclaimed.

The Torah's laws of *Shemittah* apply only to produce grown in *Eretz Yisrael*. That was why the *Shemittah* cycle could begin only when the Jews were settled in the land of Israel. They refrained from working in the fields not only every seventh year, but every 50th year as well. This 50th year is called the *Yovel* [Jubilee] year, and it, too, is mentioned in the Torah.

The *Yovel*, or Jubilee year, came after the seventh observance of the seven-year *Shemittah* cycle. When this occurred, the fields remained untended not only during the 49th year, but during the 50th year too, and the land had an extra year of rest. The next *Shemittah* cycle would then begin with the 51st year, when the Jews could again plant their fields.

The *Yovel* year had additional features besides that of a *Shemittah* year. It was a time of complete and unqualified freedom. On *Yom Kippur* of the *Yovel* year, the *shofar* was sounded in the *Sanhedrin*, and the Torah commanded the Jews to "proclaim liberty throughout the land, and to all its inhabitants." (*Vayikra 25:10*). (This phrase was inscribed on the Liberty Bell in Philadelphia to commemorate the freedom won in the American Revolution.) During the *Yovel* celebration, all signs of ownership were removed. All Jewish slaves were freed, and all the fields that had been purchased were returned to their original owners.

This reminded every man that he was not the true master of the land, nor of his fellow man.

Yovel applied only as long as all twelve tribes were settled in *Eretz Yisrael*. Sadly, that is not the case now. *Shemittah* observance, however, is still very much a part of Jewish life, as it has been for thousands of years.

The strength of that observance throughout history has varied. Often the Jews kept the *Shemittah* with a firm faith, and tried to improve their observance wherever possible. This is clear from the following story related by Ayvo in the *Gemara* (*Succah* 44b):

> I was once standing before Rabbi Eliezer Ben Rabbi Tzaddok, when a farmer came in with a question. "I own hamlets and vineyards," he said. "I hire people from the nearby villages to dig the earth around my vines during *Shemittah*. (This is allowed during *Shemittah* because it is not done to make the vines produce grapes, but in order to keep them from dying.) As payment for their work, they eat olives from my groves. But by having them take my olives as pay, I am keeping the olives away from the poor people who are entitled to them. Is it proper for my workers to take the olives?"
>
> Rabbi Eliezer answered, "No, [I'm afraid not]." (The farmer was using his *Shemittah* olives to pay his workers' salaries. That is a *business* expense, but *Shemittah* crops may be used only for food, not for business.)

The farmer accepted the decision and promised that from then on he would pay his workers from his own money and leave all the crops for the poor.

When he left, Rabbi Eliezer exclaimed, "I have lived in *Eretz Yisrael* for forty years, and I have never met a more straightforward man than this farmer."

The Jews' devotion to *Shemittah* observance was well known even to the non-Jews who sometimes ruled over them. Both Alexander the Great and Julius Caesar cancelled Jewish tax payments during the *Shemittah* year. They knew that the Jews did not raise crops throughout the year, and would therefore not have the means to supply the tax. Unfortunately, not all rulers were so kindly, as is clear from the following story, which is based on historical facts. In the *Shemittah* year of 3976 (215–216 C.E.), Rabbi Yannai proclaimed that the Jews of *Eretz Yisrael* should plant their fields because of the dangers they faced from Roman tax collectors. The only historical people in the following story are Rabbi Yannai and the Emperor Caracella; the other characters are fictitious.

Plant in Tears... Reap in Joy

Rome
8 Tammuz, 3975
My Dearest Father,
Baruch Hashem, all is well here. The ports and markets of Rome are crowded with people from all over

the world, selling and buying everything imaginable. Our wine is selling very well. The Jewish community in Rome is large and prospering, and there is not a Jew in the entire city who is not anxious to obtain wine from *Eretz Yisrael*! Furthermore, I have even sent scores of barrels up north to the Jews living in Gaul and Ashkenaz (France and Germany). We have much to be grateful for. The Emperor Marcus Aurelius Antonius Caracella is a great friend and protector of the Jews.

I long for our village of Peki'in and for our hilly farm and fields, and for the sight of Tzfas sitting high up in the mountains. The skies in Rome are not as blue as those in *Eretz Yisrael*, and the *Shechinah* (Presence of Hashem) seems so far away here. My warmest regards to Mother and my brother, Zakkai.

    Your loving son, Nachum

Peki'in
12 Av, 3975
My Beloved Son, Nachum,
We are busy day and night harvesting grapes. The hills of the Galil are covered with bursting vines. They are heavy and laden with a blessed crop; just as the Torah promised, we are harvesting a double crop this year, so that there will be enough to last through next year's Shemittah, *when the land will lay unplanted.*

Zakkai is still learning in Akraba in the yeshiva of Rabbi Yannai, but he, too, is working in the vineyards. Rabbi Yannai uses the harvest of his 400 vineyards to support the yeshiva and his students, and all of them help with the work.

The only cloud on our horizon is the Emperor's army. His soldiers are camping in Palestine — thousands and thousands of them—waiting to march northward to Parthia, where it is said great battles will soon take place. My son, do not become too enthusiastic about Emperor Caracella. He can be a cruel man—people say he has just massacred thousands of people in Alexandria. Our only true Protector is the Alm-ghty Himself. How often I thought of this three days ago during the fast of Tisha B'Av. *May we see the rebuilding of our* Bais Hamikdash *soon.*

    Your father, Yosef ben Chilkia

Rome
26 Av, 3975
Dearest Father,
As always, your words ring true. Yes, the Emperor can be a cruel man. Some say that Caracella thinks he is Alexander the Great reborn, and just as Alexander conquered Persia, Caracella will conquer Parthia.

But let us be grateful for the many privileges Caracella and his father, Severus, conferred upon the Jews. Has he not given the *Nassi* (leader of the Jews) great power and authority to govern the Jews in *Eretz Yisrael*?

By the way, perhaps it would be wise to think of setting aside a larger sum for next year's taxes, because the Emperor will need much gold to finance his Parthian adventure. Love to Mother and Zakkai.

    Your son, Nachum

Peki'in
19 Elul, 3975
My Dear Son, Nachum,
Rosh Hashanah *and the beginning of the* Shemittah *year will soon be here. It is with great trust in Hashem that we will declare everything growing in our fields* hefker *(ownerless) and put aside our farming tools for the year.*

We are well, thank G-d, but strange rumors are being circulated. They say that the emperor will demand that next year's taxes be paid in food, instead of money, to feed his army. Yet the Romans know that next year is a Shemittah *year, when we do not plant. It is difficult to believe that Caracella will insist upon such a thing after his father exempted us from payments of taxes during a* Shemittah *year. There is talk that Rabbi Yannai is considering the possibility of planting during* Shemittah. *This, of course, is hard to believe, but it just shows you what people will say when they are confused.*

Did I tell you what Rabbi Yannai did? He had an orchard ready to be harvested on Chol Hamoed *(intermediate Days of a Festival), and rather than pick the fruit—which is permissible rather than let it rot— he declared the orchard* hefker *and gave up his entire profit! Can you imagine such a man planting during* Shemittah? *Personally, I, Yosef ben Chilkia, would rather abandon my farm than desecrate the* Shemittah *year!*

A kesiva vachasima tova *to you, my son, and may Hashem watch over you and hasten your safe return to the Land of our Fathers!*

Your loving father, Yosef

Rome
6 Tishrei, 3976
My Dearest Father,
The rumors are true! Caracella is refusing tax payment of money. If the army is not well-fed while it is waiting to go to Parthia, it will destroy everything we have so painstakingly built since the destruction of Beitar eighty-three years ago. Our farms and cities, our *batei knesses* (synagogues) and yeshivos, even the *Sanhedrin* (High court) itself, will not escape the wrath of the Emperor and the Governor if the army goes wild!

Be careful, Father. Caracella can be ruthless. It is whispered that he "hastened" the death of his sick father, Severus, and all of Rome knows that he murdered his brother Geta and 20,000 of his supporters. If you abandon the farm during *Shemittah*, the Romans will simply give it to someone else to work, and you and Mother will be branded outlaws! Please, speak to Rabbi Yannai before you decide anyhting.

I spent *Rosh Hashanah* at the home of our cousin, Milka and her husband, but I sorely missed being in Peki'in! A *g'mar chasima tova* to all of you.

Your son, Nachum

Peki'in
10 Marcheshvan, 3976
Dear Nachum,
Marcheshvan is truly a bitter month for the Jewish People. Rabbi Yannai has proclaimed, "Go and plant your seed in the Sabbatical year, because of the tax-collectors!" Woe that I have lived to hear such a thing!

Zakkai told Rabbi Yannai that I refused to heed his advice, and Rabbi Yannai asked to speak to me. I was saddened to see that in Akraba they are already planting. Rabbi Yannai says it is a matter of pikuach nefesh *(life and death). He called the Roman army a restless, dangerous animal, and said if it is not well-fed our very lives will be in danger. He asked me to set an example for my neighbors and be among the first in Peki'in to plant. I don't know what to do. It is no easy matter to disregard the request of a great and holy* rav *like Rabbi Yannai, yet I have lived through ten* Shemittah *years, and never have I disturbed the peace of the land on its Shabbos. Surely G-d will provide for the Roman army in a different way. His supply of miracles is unending.*

Your father, Yosef

Rome
14 Kislev, 3976
Dearest Father,
News travels fast. Even in Rome the Jews have heard of Rabbi Yannai's decision. But Rabbi Yannai said more than you wrote. He said, "A man should not stand in a place of danger and say, "A miracle shall be performed for me." The Torah was given for us to LIVE by, and this IS a matter of life and death. Follow Rabbi Yannai's advice, I beg you. For Mother's sake, if not for your own. And for the sake of the neighbors who will follow your example. Rabbi Yannai did not only "permit" planting, he is *urging* our people to plant in order to save their lives!

And, Father, take heart. This is the month of *Chanukah*. G-d helped us once in the month of *Kislev*. Hopefully, He will come to our aid again!

Your loving son, Nachum

Peki'in
7 Shevat, 3976
Dear Nachum,
The winter is upon us in all its fury. The rains are hard and the cold is fierce. The legions are threatening mutiny if they do not receive larger food rations. And they are chopping down every tree in sight for firewood to keep warm. In Usha, soldiers broke into a house and took the stores of grain and fruit, which had been put aside for the Shemittah *year. Now they accuse us of hiding food from them. Three people were killed in Usha and others were wounded. Rabbi Yannai travels everywhere, exhorting us to plant. I do not know what to do.*

Your grieving father, Yosef

Peki'in
19 Shevat, 3976
My son,
It has been decided. We will plant in the Shemittah *year. My crops shall be watered by my tears. May Hashem have mercy on His children.*

Your father

17

Rome
Rosh Chodesh Adar, 3976
Dear Father,

I have sold all our wine in Rome. Please G-d, I am returning home next week to help you plant.

We cannot understand the ways of the Alm-ghty. The Jews in *Eretz Yisrael* are "losing" a *Shemittah*, but the Torah is eternal, and *b'ezras Hashem* (with G-d's help), we will live to keep many other *Shemittah* years.

Today is *Rosh Chodesh Adar*, a time for joy. Even your tears, Father, shall be a sign of our joy, as you yourself taught me from the words of *Tehillim*, "They who plant in tears, shall reap in joy!"

Your loving son, Nachum

The preceding story was a case of *Pikuach nefesh*, a threat to the lives of the Jews, which is why they were allowed to forego *Shemittah* observance in that instance. Unfortunately, though, there were some years in which the Jews ignored the *Shemittah* observance out of laziness or greed or lack of faith. Sages tell us that during the first 850 years that the Jews lived in *Eretz Yisrael*, they neglected to observe *Shemittah* 70 times. In accordance with the punishment of exile prescribed in the Torah, Hashem forced the Jews into exile in Bavel for 70 years. This way, the Jews were not able to tend their fields, and the land got back the 70 years of rest that were due it. When Hashem arranged for the Jews to return from this exile, they knew that they had better observe *Shemittah* from then on.

Sadly, the Jews were guilty of other misdeeds, and the *Bais Hamikdash* was demolished again, and the Jews wandered from land to land and from continent to continent in a *galus* (exile) that continues to this day. There were always Jews living in *Eretz Yisrael*, but their numbers were generally very small. Most of the land remained fallow during these *Shemittah* years, because there was almost no one to work in the fields.

In the 1800's Jews began returning to Eretz Yisrael in growing numbers. Many were forced to tend the land in order to survive. With the upsurge in farming, the question of *Shemittah* took on a new urgency. Could the Jews stop working the fields for a full year and still be able to survive?

Before we discuss some of the current methods of observing *Shemittah*, let us examine some of the basic *Shemittah* laws. These laws are very complex and intricate, and anyone wishing to know them in full must spend a long time studying them with a knowledgeable person. The following *brief* review of some of the essential laws will help us understand, somewhat, what is and isn't allowed during and after the *Shemittah* year.

Some forbidden field labors during Shemittah
Planting

Pruning

III. Shemittah Laws

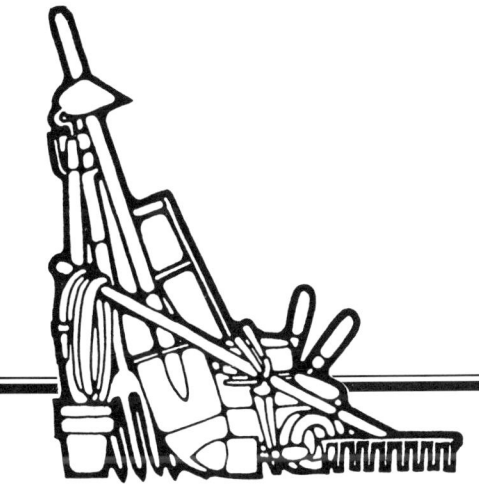

WHERE THEY APPLY

The holiness of the land of *Eretz Yisrael* makes it special, and that is why certain *mitzvos* apply only there. One of these *mitzvos* is *Shemittah*. All of the land that was part of *Eretz Yisrael* during the time of either *Bais Hamikdash* must lie fallow (not worked on) in the seventh year—the *Shemittah* year. This refers to *most* of what is today's State of Israel and to certain other adjacent areas as well.

Shemittah applies only to land in *Eretz Yisrael* owned by Jews. Crops grown on such land during *Shemittah* are forbidden. If a non-Jew grows crops in a field in *Eretz Yisrael* that is owned by non-Jews, these crops have no *Kedushas Sheviis* (holiness of the seventh year—the *Shemittah* year—as explained later) and may be eaten. This is the custom of the Jews living in Jerusalem. However, in the *yishuv hachadash*—Bnei Brak and elsewhere—the custom is to apply the laws of *Kedushas Sheviis* even to crops grown on non-Jewish farms. Circumstances must always be checked carefully. Do not assume that food sold in an Arab marketplace is always permissible, because the food might in fact have been grown in a field owned by a Jew.

The laws of *Shemittah* do not apply to crops grown outside of *Eretz Yisrael*, even if they are grown by Jews. Jews living outside of *Eretz Yisrael* must be careful that the Israeli products that they buy during and after *Shemittah* conform to the laws of *Shemittah*, as explained later.

FORBIDDEN WORK

The following field-related labors were banned by the Torah during the *Shemittah* year:

זְמִירָה   זְרִיעָה
a) Planting   b) Pruning
(*all types*)

קְצִירָה   בְּצִירָה
c) Harvesting   d) Fruit Picking

חֲרִישָׁה
e) Plowing

Shemittah begins on *Rosh Hashanah* of the *Shemittah* year, however, even in weeks just before *Shemittah*, it is forbidden to plant, but the time of this prohibition varies depending on the kind of plant as follows:

Fruit trees from the 16th of *Av* before the *Shemittah* year; non-fruit trees—from 14 days before the *Shemittah* year; all other plantings—from the 27th of *Elul* before *Shemittah*. Some authorities permit these other plantings until *erev Rosh Hashanah* preceding *Shemittah*.

Planting, pruning and plowing are prohibited the entire year of

Some forbidden field labors during Shemittah
Harvesting

Plowing

Fruit picking

Some forbidden field labors during Shemittah
Fertilizing

Spraying pesticides

One may pick a little bit of fruit at a time

Learning how the laws of Shemittah apply to flowers

Shemittah. Harvesting and fruit picking by means of the usual tools or machinery are prohibited for any produce that has *Kedushas Sheviis*, not only during *Shemittah*, but even after the *Shemittah* year. However, these crops may be taken a little bit at a time (enough for three meals) if they are not cut in the usual manner, that is, using different cutting tools, etc.

On the other hand, produce that does *not* have the holiness of *Sheviis*, may be harvested and picked the usual way even during the *Shemittah* year. For example, oranges that were formed in the sixth year but were left on the tree to get bigger and riper, may be picked in the usual way during *Shemittah*.

Besides the Torah prohibition of field-related work mentioned above, our Sages prohibited other types of field work, such as watering, fertilizing, removing stones, spraying pesticides, etc. Basically, any farm work that will cause the land to produce more or better crops is forbidden. However, you are permitted to do the types of work which were prohibited only by our Sages if it is necessary to keep the crops alive, and if this could not have been done before the *Shemittah* year. For example, you may water orchards and fields if this is needed to keep their trees and plants from dying.

The prohibitions mentioned above also apply to private gardens and houseplants in Israel. Nevertheless, houseplants (planted before *Shemittah*) may be tended in the usual way, according to some authorities, if the pot has no hole on the bottom and has a plate of metal or plastic underneath which completely separates the plant from the ground, and if the plant remains indoors or on a covered balcony. Some other restrictions apply as well.

Flowers having fragrance are to be treated like other plantings in regard to the laws of *Sefichin* and *Kedushas Sheviis* (explained later). However, it has become accepted by many that flowers not having fragrance, but which are only decorative, are not governed by the laws of *Sefichin* or *Kedushas Sheviis*. They should, however, not be planted during *Shemittah*. *All questions regarding* Shemittah *observance should be directed to a rabbinic authority*.

PROHIBITED AND PERMITTED PRODUCE

The laws of *Shemittah* apply to *all* grown food—all fruit, vegetables, grains and pulses. However, for the purpose of classification, one must distinguish between: a) ground crops which are planted anew each year, comprised of (1) vegetables (2) grains and pulses (i.e., peas and beans); and b) tree fruit which grow themselves year after year. The laws, however, are not the same for both categories.

Some crops growing in a Jewish-owned field during *Shemittah* are totally prohibited, some are totally permitted, and some are permitted, but have *halachic* restrictions governing their use, because of *Kedushas Sheviis* (the holiness of the *Shemittah* year).

A. Prohibited Produce (Sefichin)

All sorts of vegetables, grains and pulses which were planted by a Jew, or in a Jewish-owned field during

Checking the size of the roots

Checking to see if seeds began to sprout before Rosh Hashanah

the *Shemittah* year, may not be eaten. Vegetables which do not begin to sprout before the *Shemittah* year are prohibited in *Shemittah* even though they were planted before *Shemittah*.

Grains and pulses that began growing before *Shemittah* but did not reach ⅓ of their growth until the *Shemittah* year began, are prohibited. Equally prohibited are any vegetables, ground fruit (i.e., melons) or grains and pulses that grew on their own, without being planted, during *Shemittah*. This can happen in cases when plants sprouted from seeds that remained in the field during the previous year's harvest or when a seed was blown into the ground by the wind. The produce of such unintentional planting are prohibited in order to prevent untrustworthy people from planting seeds in the normal way during *Shemittah* and then claiming that these seeds fell into the ground accidentally. All of the prohibited produce mentioned above fall under the *issur* (prohibition) referred to as *Sefichin*. *Sefichin* plants must be uprooted and set aside so that they won't be used. Like other foods with *Kedushas Sheviis*, it is forbidden to destroy *Sefichin*. They must be left to rot on their own.

There are other conditions and situations where certain types of *Sefichin* may be permitted, which are not discussed here.

B. Permitted Produce
(**Not Having Kedushas Sheviis**)

All tree fruit that began to form *before* the *Shemittah* year are permitted during the *Shemittah* year. Grains and pulses that reached ⅓ of their growth *before Shemittah* are also permitted. These have *no Kedushas Sheviis* and may be harvested, picked and eaten as usual during *Shemittah*. *Terumos* and *ma'asros* must be taken from these permitted produce.

C. Permitted Produce
(**Having Kedushas Sheviis**)

All vegetables and ground fruit (i.e., melons) that began to sprout *before* the *Shemittah* year, and were gathered during the *Shemittah* year, and tree fruit that formed during the *Shemittah* year, (the prohibition of *Sefichin* does not apply to tree fruit), or grains and pulses which grew ⅓ during *Shemittah* in a field where the prohibition of *Sefichin* doesn't apply, have *Kedushas Sheviis*. They must be eaten and treated *B'kedushas Sheviis* according to the following regulations: (Each regulation is described briefly. See other sources for more in-depth explanations.)

הַפְקָרַת הַפֵּרוֹת

1) The owner of the field must make his crops available freely to every Jew. As mentioned before, *Shemittah* observance shows us that human beings are not the real owners of the land. Therefore, these crops must be freed for use by all Jews, and the landowner may not hoard them for himself. If he does, the crops may no longer be used, according to many opinions. Any Jew, including the owner of the field, may take (not in the usual manner) produce for himself and his family, but only as much as he would normally take

home to eat for a day or so. After one finishes this amount, he may take more.

אִסוּר סְחוֹרָה

2) If the owner or anyone else took the permitted amount of *Sheviis* food for himself or his family, he may sell it in private—but only under the special conditions. He may not weigh or package the food as he usually would when selling it. Also, the purchaser should not pay the money for the food at the time that he receives it because that money is *dmei Sheviis* (*Sheviis* money), which takes upon itself the holiness of *Sheviis*. Instead, one of the options is for the purchaser to buy on credit, which means that he takes the food first and agrees to pay money later. In this way, the money is not a direct payment for the food, but a payment of the debt. It is best to buy one's produce only in rabbinically supervised stores where transactions are made according to Torah law.

אָפְנֵי הַשִּׁמוּשׁ בָּהֶם

3) Foods having *Kedushas Sheviis* may be eaten only in their usual form. For instance if they are usually eaten cooked, they may not be eaten raw, or vice versa. Many other conditions are not mentioned here.

אִסוּר לְהַפְסִידָם

4) Because of their holiness, foods (including fruit cores, peels etc.) having *Kedushas Sheviis* must not be thrown away or destroyed as long as they are still edible. Instead, they must be kept in special containers until they rot. When they can no longer be eaten by humans, but are still edible for animals, they may be fed to them, but not thrown away. Only when they are not fit for either human or animal consumption may they be thrown into the garbage.

These foods may not be given to a non-Jew or exported from *Eretz Yisrael*, etc.

בְּעוּר

5) As soon as a type of produce is no longer found in a field—as when oranges are no longer growing on trees—the person who has this type of produce in his possession must peform *bi'ur*—the removal of that type of produce from his possession. He does this by first removing from his house all of the accumulated produce of that variety. For instance—all his oranges or jars of orange jam must be taken out to a public place. He brings it out to the street and in front of three Jewish men, declares that it is *hefker* (ownerless). After that has been done, anyone—both the owner and anyone else—can take the produce and use it according to the laws of *Kedushas Sheviis*. But if the owner does not perform *bi'ur* at the proper time, the food many no longer be used. The time of *bi'ur* will vary from food to food, because the growing seasons of the various foods are not the same. The rabbis of *Eretz Yisrael* publicize the dates by which *bi'ur* must be performed for each type of crop. They also publicize the dates when vegetables and fruits having *Kedushas Sheviis* will appear in the marketplace during the *She-*

mittah year and the dates until when they will be on the marketplace the following year. They also give the dates when the prohibition of *Sefichin* for vegetables, grains and pulses apply.

אוֹצַר בֵּית דִּין

6) Foods having *Kedushas Sheviis* should be bought from stores having the *Otzar Bais Din* arrangement (explained later), to avoid *Shemittah* violations.

Foods having *Kedushas Sheviis* are exempt from *terumos* and *ma'asros*.

When the *Shemittah* year is over and the eighth year begins, it does not mean that the *Shemittah* laws are no longer in force. Some food prohibitions continue past the seventh year as well, because many foods that are harvested in the eighth year grew in the seventh year. Some foods are forbidden forever. One must be careful, therefore, to check the various guides that list the dates until when the *Shemittah* food prohibitions apply and when each type of produce becomes completely permissible again. It is best to continue getting your produce from *Shemittah* supervised stores.

Leftovers must be kept in special containers until they rot.

Rabbi Kalman Kahana z"l, Rabbi of Kibbutz Chofetz Chaim, an authority on the laws of Shemittah, and a pioneer activist for Shemittah observance in modern-day Eretz Yisrael.

General view of Kibbutz Chofetz Chaim, where the laws of Shemittah are strictly observed.

IV. Shemittah: In Eretz Yisrael

During the late 1800's and early 1900's, most people thought that it was impossible to keep *Shemittah*. They could not see how a valiant but very poor people in *Eretz Yisrael* could abandon their fields for a whole year in the face of poverty, disease and Arab attacks.

Some rabbis formulated a method to avoid the difficulties of *Shemittah*. Since *Shemittah* does not apply to land owned by a non-Jew, the rabbis arranged for the sale of Jewish-owned fields in *Eretz Yisrael* to an Arab for the *Shemittah* year only. The conditions of this *heter* (lenient authorization) were that non-Jews would work the fields during this period and that the *heter* would only be temporary. After the *Shemittah* year, the Rabbinate would buy back the land. While some Jews relied on the *heter*, others claimed that, "After all, if we are privileged to live in *Eretz Yisrael*, we have an obligation to preserve its *mitzvos* despite all hardships." The *heter* is still in use today in some circles.

Throughout the years that the *heter* has been in existence, it was opposed by many rabbis, including the *Ridbaz*, Rabbi Yaakov David Willowski, זצ״ל, and the *Chazon Ish*, Rabbi Avraham Yeshayahu Karelitz, זצ״ל. They argued that it is forbidden to sell any part of *Eretz Yisrael* to a non-Jew, and therefore, for this and other reasons, the laws of *Shemittah* apply to the land even if such a "sale" is made. They insisted that the laws of *Shemittah* must be kept as they always were without the *heter*, despite the difficulties involved.

In 1933, Kibbutz Chofetz Chaim was founded by seven pioneering farmers, and named in honor of the great Sage who had died that year. A *kibbutz* is a collective farm, in which the property is owned by everyone and the work is shared equally. There were already many *kibbutzim* in the country, but Kibbutz Chofetz Chaim was special. Founded by members of Poalei Agudath Israel, it was among the first collective farms run by religious Jews who were fully committed to the laws and ideals of the Torah. The founders made up their minds to run their farms strictly according to *halachah*. Led by their famous rabbi, Rabbi Kalman Kahana, and with the guidance of rabbis like the *Chazon Ish*, and the technology of religious scientists and agronomists, they developed ways to keep their farms functioning without violating the laws of Shabbos or *Shemittah*.

Once during a *Shemittah* year, the famous Rabbi of Ponevez, Rabbi Yosef Shlomo Kahaneman, זצ״ל, paid a visit to Kibbutz Chofetz Chaim to see first hand how the

Rabbi Yosef Shlomo Kahaneman, zt"l, Rabbi and Rosh Yeshiva of Ponevez.

The Ponevez Yeshiva

courageous farmers were keeping *Shemittah*. As soon as he arrived on the kibbutz, he threw himself on the ground, kissed it, and with a voice choked with tears and emotion he called out, "Gut Shabbos to you Mother Earth, Gut Shabbos to you." (The Torah refers to the *Shemittah* year as a Shabbos for Hashem.) He then went over to tree after tree and said, "Gut Shabbos to you my dear tree, Gut Shabbos to you."

Among other religious *kibbutzim* and *moshavim* (settlements), where farmers are complying strictly with the laws of *Shemittah* are: Komemiyus, Sha'alvim, Yesodot, Kfar Gideon, Beit Chelkiyah and Mattityahu. Today, thousands of observant Jews live on these settlements. They are proof that those who base their lives on *halachah* can not only survive, but can also thrive.

Members of some of these religious *kibbutzim* and *moshavim* organized the "Institute for Agricultural Research According to the Torah." The Institute's purpose was to find strictly *halachic* ways of using modern technology and scientific discoveries to deal with farming problems. For instance, the Institute developed an electric milking machine for milking cows on Shabbos; it turns on and off automatically. The Institute also investigated ways of helping religious farmers cope with the demands of the *Shemittah* year, and emerged with several successful procedures.

Halachah states that one may not plant crops in the *soil* during the *Shemittah* year. However, there is nothing wrong with growing crops in materials other than soil. Therefore, the Institute developed "hydroponics," an ingenious method of growing vegetables in shallow concrete tanks filled with water and underlined with gravel beds. It is especially effective in producing tomatoes and lettuce. In fact, the technique proved so successful that non-religious *kibbutzim* copied it. Hydroponics is not used widely anymore, but it was the first example of a scientific breakthrough in the field of *Shemittah* observance.

Another procedure developed by the Institute is early planting. In preparing for the *Shemittah* year, the religious settlements plan far ahead. During the sixth year of the *Shemittah* cycle, they plant early, and they plant more than they immediately need. The extra produce is safely stored away, and can be used without any problems during the *Shemittah* year. In fact, the Institute found a way to grow enough cotton for two years during the sixth year. The farmers can sell this extra produce during the *Shemittah* year, and thereby stay somewhat economically secure.

HELPING FARMERS OVER THE HURDLE:
Special Funds and Encouragement

When Yosef was Pharoah's viceroy in Egypt, he did not rest during the years of plenty. Instead, he had the Egyptians store up grain to use during the seven years of famine. Some farmers in *Eretz Yisrael* use similar strategies and set up a *Shemittah* fund called the *Otzar Hashemittah*. During each of the first six years of each *Shemittah* cycle, many

Some religious settlements where the laws of Shemittah are strictly observed

Beit Chelkiyah

Komemiyus

Kfar Gideon

Yesodot

Hydroponics—growing vegetables in shallow concrete
tanks filled with water and underlined with gravel beds

A successful cotton crop

Discussing plans for the Shemittah year

An on-the-field training course in the laws of Shemittah, for rabbis.

religious *kibbutzim* and *moshavim* set aside a certain amount of money. This money is invested for use during the *Shemittah* year. Then, the saved up money is distributed to the farmers to help them make up for some of their loss of income.

However, their main source of financial support during this difficult period comes from fellow Jews throughout the world, through special *Shemittah* funds, such as the *Keren Hashemittah* and the *Keren Hasheviis*.

An organization which is active in encouraging and teaching farmers to keep the laws of *Shemittah* properly is the National Center of *Shemittah* Observing Farmers. Its representatives travel around the country offering information on the laws of *Shemittah* and offering funding and overall encouragement to farmers, so that they can endure the difficulties of the *Shemittah* year.

Today, some 4,000 farmers in over 180 agricultural settlements, observe the laws of *Shemittah*, and this number is growing from *Shemittah* to *Shemittah*.

Probably the most important factor of all in keeping these farmers from despair is their trust. Their trust in Hashem is strong, and they trust Hashem's promise that He will watch over those who observe the *Shemittah* year faithfully. These farmers are not at all surprised at the remarkable success stories that have emerged from their *Shemittah* experience—and there have been quite a number of them.

Consider what has happened at Komemiyus, an Agudath Israel *moshav* in southern Israel. It was established in 1949 by religious settlers who bravely defended the area during Israel's war with the Arabs in 1948. They decided to stay and to devote their energies to farming the land in accordance with *halachah*, including the laws of the *Shemittah* year. They were ready and willing to do so, and their trust has been rewarded.

For instance, in 5713 (1953) the farmers of Komemiyus refused to plant wheat from seed that had grown during the previous year, a *Shemittah* year. Instead, they searched all around for seed that had been left over from the year before *Shemittah*. The only such seeds that they could find looked spoiled and wormy. Experienced farmers from other *kibbutzim* told them that the seeds were worthless. The farmers of Komemiyus went to their spiritual leader, the late great Rabbi Binyamin Mendelson זצ"ל, who told them to plant the seeds anyway and have *bitachon* (trust in Hashem). Despite the warnings of others, they followed their Rav's advice. The *Shemittah* year that they had just observed had been a year plagued by drought. The summer crop planted by non-*Shemittah* observing farmers did not grow well—and when plentiful rains began to fall in the eighth year, it was too late for the non-religious settlements' parched crops; the rain completely ruined those crops. On the other hand, Komemiyus, with its "wormy seed" had near record crops during the eighth year.

In the next *Shemittah* year, 5719 (1959), two extraordinary developments occurred. Two years earlier,

Representatives of the National Center of Shemittah Observing Farmers, originating in Moshav Komemiyus, encouraging farmers to keep Shemittah.

The jeep used to travel around the country encouraging farmers to keep Shemittah.

The march is on to encourage local farmers to keep Shemittah.

Rabbi Binyamin Mendelson, zt"l, the legendary Rabbi of Komemiyus and authority on the laws of Shemittah.

Rabbi Yitzchak Hutner, zt"l, Rosh Yeshiva Rabbeinu Chaim Berlin–Gur Aryeh, on a visit to Moshav Komemiyus, in the Shemittah year 5733.

Rabbi Elya Svei (second from left), Rosh Yeshiva of Philadelphia, on a tour of Moshav Komemiyus. On his right is Rabbi Menachem Mendel Mendelson, Rabbi of Komemiyus and on his left is Rabbi Avraham Kliers.

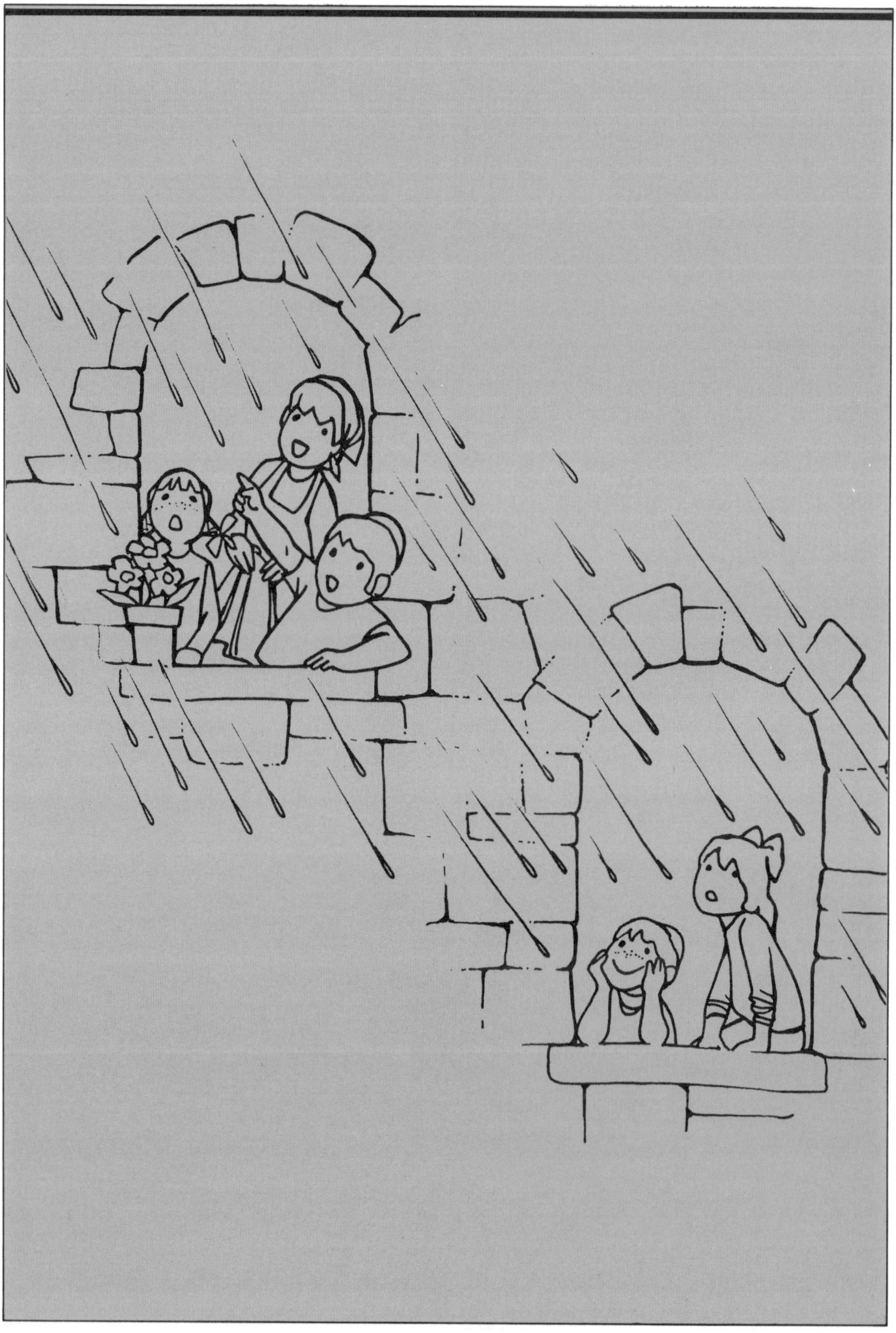

the government's Ministry of Agriculture had planted an orchard in Komemiyus. During the *Shemittah* year, the farmers of Komemiyus left the orchard untended, and the inspectors from the Ministry were very upset. "How could the farmers of Komemiyus neglect their land like this?" they demanded! But the next year, the inspectors' anger changed to amazement. Eleven non-religious settlements near Komemiyus had tended their orchards during the *Shemittah* year, yet afterwards, the *untended* orchard in Komemiyus was in better condition than any of the others.

Then there was the matter of the locusts. In that same year, the South was hit hard by a plague of locusts which swarmed from one area to another, devouring every growing thing in sight. They had ruined nearby farms and were directly on their way to Komemiyus. The land in Komemiyus had, of course, not been plowed and planted, but it was being used as pasture ground for the *moshav*'s animals. The farmers were expecting the worst and were wondering what to do if the locusts destroyed all the grass in the pasture. Just as the locusts were about to reach Komemiyus, they suddenly changed direction and bypassed the settlement completely.

In the following year, other stories emerged. Government records showed that Komemiyus had yielded three times as much produce in the year before *Shemittah* as in previous years. Even though they did not have much fresh vegetables during the *Shemittah* period, the children of Komemiyus were found to be healthier during the *Shemittah* year than children from non-religious settlements. The next year, though, their health level was the same as the other children, showing that the seventh year had been a special one.

In 5739 (1979), when the farmers needed extra rain because it was the year before *Shemittah* and additional crops had to be raised, there was a drought in the south. All the settlements near Komemiyus that do not observe *Shemittah* had a water shortage. But Komemiyus had been blessed with 300 *more* cubic meters of rain than in the year before.

The year 5746–47 (1986) also saw a miracle happen throughout *Eretz Yisrael*. As they do every seventh year, the farmers who keep *Shemittah* planted their seeds a few weeks before *Rosh Hashanah*. As long as those seeds sprouted roots before *Rosh Hashanah*, the crops would be permitted to be used during *Shemittah*. But the two years before were drought years in Israel, years with very little rain. The ground was so dry that the seeds couldn't sprout. And it *never* rains in *Eretz Yisrael* before *Rosh Hashanah*. But — to almost everyone's amazement — that year it rained and poured a few days before *Rosh Hashanah*! Those poor dry little seeds began to grow and grow.

Afterwards, there was more rain than usual. The result was that the farmers who do not observe *Shemittah* found it very hard to plow because the land was wet and muddy. The *Shemittah*-observing farmers had unusually good crops because, for them, the rains came at exactly

The animals and fowl must be fed

the right time.

The Torah's assurances that the *Shemittah* keepers' trust in Hashem would be rewarded has come true.

Chazal (our Rabbis of blessed memory) compare *Shemittah* to *Chol Hamoed* (the intermediate days of the holidays). In truth, life in religious settlements during the *Shemittah* year closely resembles *Chol Hamoed*. During these intermediate days of *Yom Tov*, we do only necessary work, and devote the rest of the time to Hashem. In the same way, during *Shemittah*, farmers on religious settlements carry out basic labor like feeding the animals and irrigating the land to keep the crops alive. Otherwise, there is a spirit of *Yom Tov*. In *kibbutz* Sha'alvim, the members figured out that during *Shemittah*, each person would work about 150 hours less in the fields. They therefore set up special classes and study sessions so that they could learn an additional 150 hours of Torah during the year. In this way, they gained almost nineteen full eight-hour days of Torah study. This is how Jews fulfill the true spirit of *Shemittah*.

Jewish non-farmers who live in Israeli cities also have to make adjustments during *Shemittah*. A certain number of them—those who deal in agricultural produce—have to worry about earning a living. *All* Jews must be careful to use only permitted produce that was not grown, harvested or sold improperly. One way to do this is by shopping only at food stores that are supervised by the *Va'ad Hashemittah* (Rabbinical Committee for *Shemittah* observance). These stores carry food that was neither grown nor harvested during *Shemittah* in violation of *halachah*. Instead, the produce comes from a variety of sources, including the following: (a) the *Otzar Bais Din* which, as explained below, takes over the produce from the farms on behalf of the community; (b) farmland owned by Arabs who grow their own crops during *Shemittah*; and (c) food imported from other countries.

Otzar Bais Din

As you know, in most years crops are planted and harvested twice a year in *Eretz Yisrael*—winter crops are harvested in the spring and summer crops are usually planted after *Succos*. But during *Shemittah* the winter crop must be planted early, before *Rosh Hashanah*, and the summer crops which would normally be planted in the summer of the *Shemittah* year cannot be planted at all, so there will be no fall harvest after *Shemittah* ends. This is one example of how *Shemittah* affects two years.

What happens then with the crops which were planted before *Shemittah* and are ready to be harvested? The farmers cannot harvest or sell them because the Torah forbids this and the crops are now *hefker* (ownerless) and belong to all Jews. Are they left therefore just to rot away in the fields? Not at all. In the *Tosefta* we are told that in years gone by, in order to help and provide the people with food during *Shemittah* in a permissible way (to avoid *Shemittah* violations)—after all, not everybody lives next to a field or garden where he can go out

Children are taught to be extra careful with their leftovers

A supervised Shemittah produce store

and pick for himself—the *Bais Din* (Rabbinical Court) in each town hired workers who collected and stored fruit and vegetables, and then distributed them to everyone in town who came and asked for them. This arrangement is referred to as *Otzar Bais Din*—the Storehouse of the Rabbinical Court.

Nowadays as well, when *Shemittah* arrives and the farmers cannot harvest and sell their crops, they turn them over to the *Bais Din* which is allowed to do the harvesting and selling on behalf of the entire Jewish community. The *Bais Din* does not buy the crops from the farmers, since this is forbidden. Through the *Otzar Bais Din* arrangement, the farmers themselves, or other workers appointed by the *Bais Din*, harvest the crops for the *Bais Din* (in the usual manner) and have them delivered to special *Shemittah* supervised stores where they are made available to *Shemittah* observers at low prices, just enough to cover the *Bais Din*'s expenses. The *Bais Din* charges only for the work the farmers or workers did, and for their expenses—but they do not charge for the crops and do not make a profit. Supervised stores are clearly marked in most cities and towns.

Religious Jews shop for produce only in supervised stores during the *Shemittah* year and the year after, until the new permitted produce arrives. They also have to make sure when eating in restaurants and at other people's homes that the food comes from supervised stores.

Israeli children in religious schools are given intensive preparations for *Shemittah* observance. They are taught to be careful with the food that they bring to school, and to avoid dropping any food during lunch or recess. Some students learn about the practical aspects of *Shemittah* by planting special gardens before the *Shemittah* year. These gardens are then transferred over to the *Otzar Bais Din*.

It isn't always easy living by these *halachos* (Torah laws). Nevertheless, hundreds of thousands of Jews in Israel—and outside Israel—today manage to do it. In this way, they're keeping the holiness of the land alive.

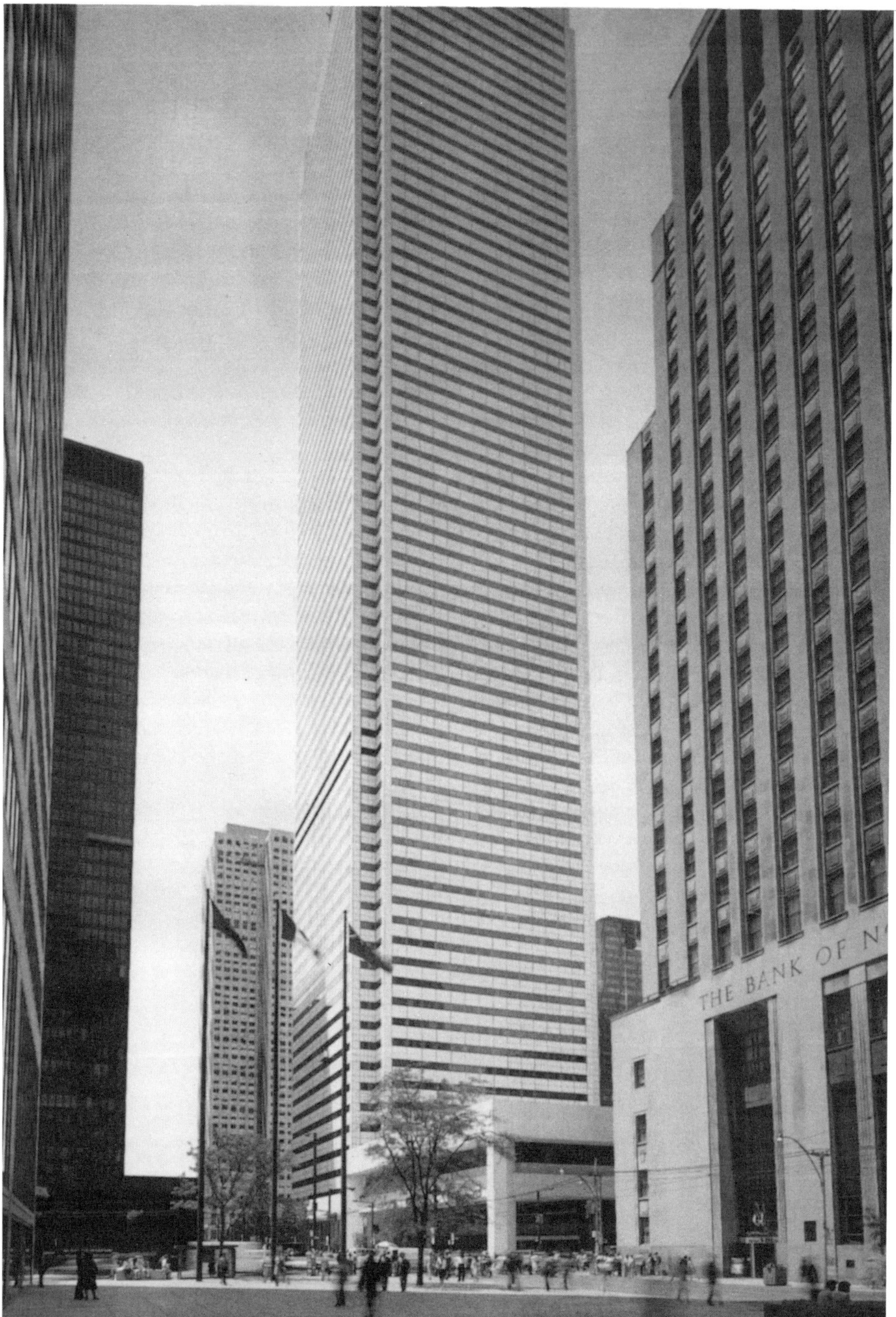
THE BANK OF N

V: Shemittah Outside Eretz Yisrael

Those who live outside *Eretz Yisrael* might think that the *Shemittah* laws have nothing to do with them. After all, they don't have to worry about not working the land, or about not buying or selling locally grown crops. Still, even Jews in *chutz la'aretz* (outside of *Eretz Yisrael*) have to be careful.

Many people in America and throughout the world buy Israeli-made products. That is fine during most years, if they meet the regular *halachic* requirements for Israeli products, such as the taking of *terumos* and *ma'asros*, etc. In the *Shemittah* year, however, and in the years immediately following, there are other problems. The Israeli produce may have been grown, harvested or sold during *Shemittah* contrary to *halachah*. One must therefore avoid buying or eating Israeli products during these years, unless he is absolutely certain that they are useable according to Torah law.

These precautions apply not only to such products as oranges and grapes, but to other things as well. Canned foods, jellies, frozen foods, candies, pet food and medicines, etc., often have ingredients that were grown in *Eretz Yisrael* and they must be carefully checked. Sweet-smelling flowers that come from Israel cannot be used either. Therefore, even Jews living outside the Holy Land must always be on the alert during this time. They, too, have an obligation to avoid *Shemittah* problems, and to maintain the holiness of this unique year.

פְּרוֹזְבּוֹל/PROZBOL

The creditor appears before judges and declares:

מוֹסְרַנִי לָכֶם (names of the judges), הַדַּיָּנִין שֶׁבְּמָקוֹם (name of place), שֶׁכָּל חוֹב שֶׁיֵּשׁ לִי שֶׁאֶגְבֶּנּוּ כָּל זְמַן שֶׁאֶרְצֶה.

I submit to you (names of the judges), *the judges who are in* (name of place), *that every debt due me, I will be allowed to collect whenever I wish.*

The judges sign the following document and present it to the creditor:

בְּמוֹתַב תְּלָתָא כַּחֲדָא הֲוֵינָא כַּד אָתָא קֳדָמָנָא הַמַּלְוֶה וְאָמַר לְפָנֵינוּ — מוֹסְרַנִי לָכֶם (name of creditor) הַדַּיָּנִין שֶׁבְּמָקוֹם (name of place) שֶׁכָּל חוֹב (names of the judges) שֶׁיֵּשׁ לִי שֶׁאֶגְבֶּנּוּ כָּל זְמַן שֶׁאֶרְצֶה. וְעַל זֶה בָּאנוּ עַל הַחֲתִימָה הַיּוֹם (Hebrew date).

חתימות הדיינים: _____
_____
_____

We were sitting as a unit of three when (name of creditor) *the creditor came before us and said — I submit to you* (names of the judges), *the judges who are in* (name of place), *that every debt due me, I will be allowed to collect whenever I wish. Upon this we affix our signature on this day* (Hebrew date).

Signatures of judges _____
_____
_____

Reproduced courtesy of Mesorah Publications

VI. Shemittas Kesafim: Financial Shemittah

THE PROZBOL

There is another feature of the *Shemittah* year that has nothing to do with the land or crops, but which involves Jews all over—not only in *Eretz Yisrael*. Through two direct commands, the Torah tells us that all debts owed to another Jew at the close of the *Shemittah* year are automatically forgiven. All debts are null and void. This is referred to as *Shemittas Kesafim* (financial *Shemittah*) and it impresses upon us the fact that we are not the true lasting owners of anything.

The great leader, Hillel HaZakein, who lived over 2,000 years ago, observed that this law of financial *Shemittah* made people afraid to lend money to one another just before and during the *Shemittah* year. Lenders were afraid that the borrowers would not pay back in time and the debts would be cancelled. Hillel found a way to make it easier for borrowers to get the money they needed. The *halachah* is that only private debts are forgiven, but not depts belonging to a *Bais Din* (Rabbinical court). Therefore, Hillel introduced the *Prozbol*, a legal document through which a lender signs over his debts to the *Bais Din*. Since the debts now belong to the *Bais Din*, they are not forgiven and the *Bais Din* simply permits the lender to collect his debts as an agent of the court. In this way he will no longer fear to lend money during this period. So, thanks to Hillel HaZakein, both the lender and the borrower are protected. The *Prozbol* is very much in use today as it has been since the time of Hillel HaZakein.

Rabbi Avraham Yeshayahu Karelitz, zt"l, The "Chazon Ish," world renowned Torah authority and architect of Shemittah observance procedures in modern-day Eretz Yisrael.

VII: Conclusion

In a world that has great respect for science and "reality," and downplays faith and trust in Hashem, it is hard to observe the *Shemittah* laws. It takes courage to ignore one's crops for a whole year and great trust to rely on Hashem's promise that all will be well. But courageous people of trust are doing it. Here is how the *Chazon Ish* described the feelings of a religious farmer regarding *Shemittah*:

> I am a farmer who toils hard for a living. Now I faced the onset of the *Shemittah* year, and—as a descendant of a stubborn, stiff necked people—I became obsessed with the idea of stubbornly observing the *Shemittah* according to *halachah*. I was alone, isolated—a mockery to all my neighbors. "What? Shall we neither plant nor harvest? You can't fight reality!"
>
> But my stubbornness stood by me. Even though every person with common sense "knows" that it is "impossible" to observe the *Shemittah*—and that its laws are only for people who have enough grain in their silos for three years—that today's generations are not like the older generations, nevertheless, half a *Shemittah* year is gone and reality is favoring me.
>
> I planted everything before *Rosh Hashanah* of the sixth year, and in the seventh year I stayed put, neither plowing nor planting. The produce of the sixth year that grew into the seventh, I treat with the holiness of *Shemittah* and eat with the holiness of *Shemittah*. Into the next half year I look forward to making peace with reality—or better said, reality will make peace with me.
>
> My neighbors who ridicule me plowed and planted during the seventh year. But reality fought them with a howling fury and ruined their crops with its great rainstorms and powerful downpours.
>
> Now, from those who have ruled leniently and permit work on *Shemittah*, I beg forgiveness for I am guilty of having disobeyed their ruling. I pray, though, that they will re-examine the entire matter, and come to the understanding that the Torah's ways are eternal and the keeping of *Shemittah* is possible for anyone who desires it. *(Translated freely from the Hebrew version in* Kovetz Igros *of the* Chazon Ish.*)*

Indeed, today's heroes are the farmers who have the courage and the will to observe *Shemittah*. Let us pray that in their merit, all Jews will soon be able to live and keep *mitzvos* in *Eretz Yisrael*, under Hashem's merciful protection.

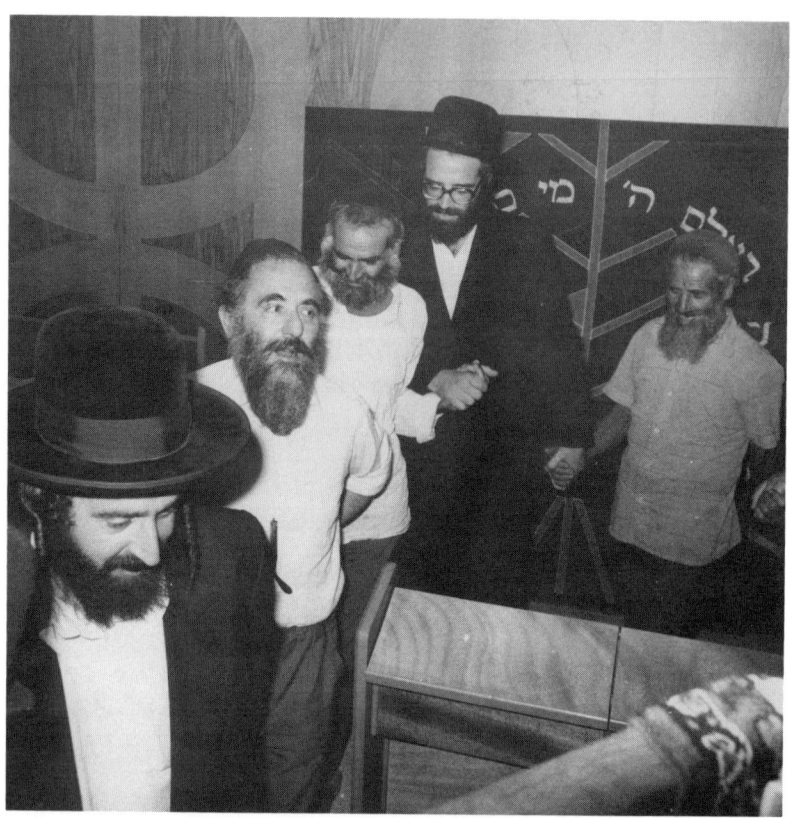

Shemittah-keeping farmers rejoice along with rabbis on being able to fulfill Hashem's commandment to observe the mitzvos of Shemittah.

A painting of the "Shivas Haminim," by Nachum ben Yehuda Tzvi, a"h.

VIII. Questions About Shemittah

1) What are the Torah sources for *Shemittah*?
2) What activities does the Torah specifically mention which are prohibited during *Shemittah*?
3) What are some of the purposes and lessons of the *Shemittah* year?
4) How should a Jew view possessions? Are riches good or bad?
5) Why are we commanded to observe Shabbos? In what ways are *Shemittah* and Shabbos similar?
6) To what use can the free time during Shabbos and *Shemittah* be put?
7) According to Rabbi Samson R. Hirsch, what impression was *Shemittah* observance supposed to convey?
8) What obvious question does the Torah raise on behalf of those who observe *Shemittah*, and what is the answer given?
9) What is the Torah's punishment for those who do not observe *Shemittah*, and why is this fitting?
10) When was *Yovel* observed, and in what way is it similar to *Shemittah*?
11) Why did Rabbi Eliezer Ben Rabbi Tzadok consider the farmer the most straightforward man he ever met?
12) In the story "Plant in Tears, Reap in Joy," explain the views of the father and Rabbi Yannai.
13) Why has there been renewed interest and concern about *Shemittah* during the last hundred years?
14) Where does *Shemittah* apply, and where not?
15) When may fruits and vegetables be eaten during the seventh year, and when not?
16) What is meant by *Sefichin*?
17) What is meant by *Kedushas Sheviis*?
18) What special regulations involve produce having *Kedushas Sheviis*? Explain five of these regulations (not *Otzar Bais Din*).
19) Why can't all foods grown or sold in Israel be eaten immediately at the beginning of the eighth year?
20) List some of the field-related labors which are prohibited during *Shemittah*. a) Those prohibited by the Torah. b) Those prohibited by the Sages.
21) What problems does a religious settlement face, and how have the settlements tried to solve them?
22) What is the method of hydroponics, and why can it be used during *Shemittah*?
23) What preparations do observant farmers make in the sixth year to get ready for *Shemittah*?
24) How does the *Otzar Bais Din* arrangement work? Why is it permissible?
25) In what ways was the faith of those in religious *kibbutzim* rewarded? Can you think of any similar examples of rewarded faith from your life or the lives of those you know?
26) In what ways is the *Shemittah* year like *Chol Hamoed*?
27) How do stores supervised by the *Va'ad Hashemittah* get produce that can be sold?
28) Why is there a need for separate garbage containers during *Shemittah*?
29) What are the effects of the *Shemittah* year on Jews inside and outside of *Eretz Yisrael*? What accommodations must they make?
30) Explain *Shemittas Kesafim*. What is the reasoning behind the *Prozbol*?

NOTES

לשנה־הבאה־בירושלים־